The Beginner's

Easy Tips and T   g

Houseplants in Your Home

Healthy Gardening Series

Dueep Jyot Singh

Mendon Cottage Books

JD-Biz Publishing

Download Free Books!

http://MendonCottageBooks.com

Disclaimer

The information is this book is provided for informational purposes only. It is not intended to be used and medical advice or a substitute for proper medical treatment by a qualified health care provider. The information is believed to be accurate as presented based on research by the author.

The contents have not been evaluated by the U.S. Food and Drug Administration or any other Government or Health Organization and the contents in this book are not to be used to treat cure or prevent disease.

The author or publisher is not responsible for the use or safety of any diet, procedure or treatment mentioned in this book. The author or publisher is not responsible for errors or omissions that may exist.

Warning

The Book is for informational purposes only and before taking on any diet, treatment or medical procedure, it is recommended to consult with your primary health care provider.

Check out some of the other Health Learning Series books at Amazon.com

Gardening Series on Amazon

Health Learning Series on Amazon

Download Free Books!

http://MendonCottageBooks.com

Table of Contents

Introduction

Millenniums ago, a man deciding to build a garden was fortunate because he had all that land right outside his door. All he had to do is clear out a piece of land, and mark it with a boundary wall. After that, he could go hunting for attractive looking plants in the wild, and bring them back home. With a little bit of care and cherishing, he would soon have a tame garden of his own.

But today, a large number of us are not so fortunate. Space is at a premium. Concrete jungles have taken the place of what was once nature's backyard. And that is why man is looking for easy options to bring beautiful greenery inside his limited space.

And so this book is for all those, who want to know more about indoor plants, how to grow them, how to take care of them, which are the best plant varieties which flourish indoors and tips and techniques with which you can enjoy not only a relaxing hobby, but also greenery around you.

Until just after the Second World War, indoor household plants were limited to ferns, palms, and potted plants, which flowered in season. Surely plants like aspidistras were also popular for interior decoration but soon more and more wide-ranging varieties and species of foliage parted plants began to be known to keen gardeners.

This change is due chiefly to the architects who designed postwar buildings on severe lines. Gone were the rambling houses with huge gardens. Strictly utilitarian designs were utilized by architects to design these houses and flats.

Frankly speaking most of them were chicken coops. The introduction of houseplants in a large variety of colors and fonts provided a flash of color to those austere and severe designs. You could relieve the simplicity and the austerity of the home by growing houseplants indoors.

Thanks to the improved heating and lighting systems, many varieties which were once grown in hot houses, greenhouses and conservatories would now flourish indoors as houseplants. There are many plants which are easier to grow, and last for several years.

How to Choose Houseplants

When choosing the right plants, consider first their habit, shape, coloring and texture. This is going to be in relation to the position they will be occupying in the rooms and in relation to each other.

For a group of plants, choose a tall specimen to give height. You can have a column over which a climbing variety flourishes and clings. Several shrub and bushy varieties are going to add more range to your choice. Trailing varieties can cascade over the edges of containers.

Also aim for good contrasts in leaf color and shape. Try subtle and fresh Greenleaf varieties for single specimens in key positions.

Use multiple while brackets rather than the type that holds a single plant to allow plenty of scope for contrast and grouping.

Temperature

When choosing the best plants for your house, you would need to see the temperature of the rooms. If you like living in a hothouse atmosphere, there are many plants which were definitely going to wilt, while others will flourish. That is why it is extremely important that you consider the temperature of the room in which the plants are going to live.

If the night temperature falls between 7 to 10°C, choose only the tolerant kinds of plants. That is because you are going to possibly switch off the central heating in that part of the house, while you rest during the night.

If the minimum night temperature can be maintained between 10 to 20°C, you can use intermediate plants. At higher night temperatures, the delicate varieties are going to flourish.

Humidity

Humidity and temperature are linked. The amount of moisture in the air is relatively greater at lower temperatures. Thanks to modern heating, we can get plenty of warmth in our rooms, but this often dries the atmosphere. Therefore it is important to people lines out of the range of any radiation source. This is going to be a source of dry heat. This could be and include electric fires and coal or gas fires in the winter.

Sometime in the sun is good depending on the season and variety.

Never place a plant directly over the source of dry heat such as a radiator or a heat convector. I remember a friend of mine who really loved warming herself in front of a heat radiator, especially in the winters. You would consider that to be hibernating in front of the source of heat, and naturally she wanted her indoor plants to enjoy that same warmth. She was definitely indignant when I said "Poor plants".

I had to give her a botanical lesson, telling her all about how all that heat would be detrimental to the health of her plants. Oh, she knew better. It was only then they started wilting, that she suddenly began to think that possibly I was right.

I also told her that whenever she wanted to sit in front of the radiator, she needed to put a bowl of water so that the atmosphere did not dry out completely and there was still some moisture left in the air. I do not go to her house anymore, because I am certain she expects me to say I told you so especially with her skin drying out in the winter, and the majority of her indoor plants dying in the "heat"!

All houseplants preferred humidity and the delicate ones must have it to grow and thrive. Naturally, a home cannot be turned into a steaming jungle, but plants can be help in many ways without interfering with your own personal comfort.

An easy way to provide humidity is to occasionally spray over the leaves with tepid water. This is done by using an old perfume spray bottle or something similar. You can sponge the leaves, both above and below with this tepid water and a sponge.

Fresh air is not essential to houseplants, but you may want to open the windows on a damp and mildly sunny day. This is going to raise the humidity and also disperse the harmful stale air which has been increasingly growing in your closed shut chicken coop.

Make sure that your plants are not placed in draughts. Just imagine you to be your household plant left out in the wind without any recourse to shelter. Plants are living things. Treat them the way you would want you to be treated in extremes of climates.

Another means of providing humidity is to place a 1 inch deep layer of small pebbles in the bottom of a shallow tray or a saucer. Fill this with water to just below the surface of the pebbles and stand the plant in its container on the pebbles.

When you water the plant, the surplus will drain through to the pebble base. It is going to evaporate to create the humid microclimate which the plant needs.

Take care that the plant does not stay or stand with its roots in water.

Different Types of Containers

The best method of providing and conserving humidity is to group the plants in a container. You can use a trough or a bowl. In fact, one of my friends used a large copper container with great success, because it was an unusual antique container, with plenty of nice plants growing in it.

Fill the container up with moist peat and plunge the plants into the peat up to the rim of their pots. Keeps the plants in their containers so that they can be fed and watered, according to their own individual requirements.

Keep the peat in the container moist. The moisture will then evaporate slowly forming a humid microclimate around the plants which will tend to form an umbrella of leaves over the peat to prevent the moisture from evaporating too rapidly.

To provide humidity for a single plant, find a container with a larger diameter than that of the box and moist peat in the space between the two.

Light

Light is an important factor regulating plant growth and the closer natural conditions can be simulated, the greater will be the success in growing houseplants. Many varieties originate from the floors of great tropical forests, where the sunlight is filtered through the canopy of branches and leaves overhead.

That is why most of the houseplants are going to prefer semi shade or shade.

In the winter, the canopy of the deciduous forests shed all their leaves and more, though less intense light can reach the floor of the forest.

That is why in the winter, when the days are short, you can move your houseplants nearer to a window because they need all the light they can get.

Generally speaking, plants with green leaves prefer a shaded position and many will be able to tolerate dark corners.

Multicolored leaves require more light to preserve their leaf color. So no houseplant with variegated and colored leaves, except Mother-In-Law's Tongue – you're going to get the scientific names for the common names given in this book in the Appendix. – can survive happily if you allow it to stand in the sun for long periods of time.

That is why a sunny window is not an ideal position for houseplants, unless the sunlight is filtered by net curtains or a Venetian blind.

Green houses containing houseplants should be heavily shaded in the spring and summer as a protection against strong sunlight.

Remove all the shading during the autumn and the winter. When the shading is of a type that is sprayed onto the glass outside it has renewed after heavy rain storms.

You may want to use photographic light meters as a means to check the intensity of the light reaching the leaves of houseplants.

http://www.ebay.com/sch/i.html?_trksid=p2050601.m570.l1313&_nkw=phot ographic+light+meters&_sacat=0&_from=R40

This link has prices ranging from yes, USD.99 to three figures. So perhaps you may strike lucky.

This is of course an option for all those people who do not have indoor garden lighting bulbs. So if you take your light meter outside and it reads 22, in full sunlight, 12-14 is good for green plants indoors. If you are growing colored leaves, or variegated varieties, indoors, 14 to 16 is an excellent range and 9 to 10 for the varieties that need heavy shade.

These readings are just intended to be a simple guide and naturally are not as accurate as those required by scientists. There are plenty of companies manufacturing indoor lighting bulbs, which can keep your plants happy in the shade.

Watering your plants

Don't overwater

The correct amount of watering is of supreme importance, and is largely responsible for success and failure with houseplants.

There are no cheap or readily available instruments for measuring the water content of the soil in a pot, as far as I know, but I water them by rule of hand. Sprinkle water on them slowly. As long as the water is being absorbed by the soil, well and good.

The moment it starts overflowing out of the holes, it means the soil has reached saturation point. Do not allow the water to stand.

You may want to ask experienced gardeners and horticulturists in the vicinity about their tips for watering plants. With experience, one can quickly tell from the weight of the pot whether the soil is dry or wet. A sharp rap on the side of the pot with your knuckles will confirm this. If the sound produced is a hollow ringing sound, the soil is dry. If you hear a dull thud the soil is wet and you need not water it yet.

This method, however, is only applicable to Clay pots. For plastic parts, you will have to lift them up and estimate the weight.

Another method is to check the color of the surface soil. When it is wet, it should be black or dark in color. When the soil dries out, it becomes grayish white.

After that, you can also try the time-tested touch method. Press the tips of your fingers into the topsoil. Now you can learn whether it is wet or soggy, moist or dry or hard just by the resistance offered by the compost. The two extremes of wet and dry soil should always be avoided. The ideal should be an intermediate evenly moist condition.

The amount of water required by houseplants changes with the season and even between one home and another. During the period of vigorous growth in spring and summer, houseplants require plenty of water, and the soil should not be allowed to dry out too much between watering.

In the autumn when growth slows down watering should be reduced and care should be taken not to over water your plants.

Through the winter, particularly during cold weather, the greatest care should be taken as the plants have almost ceased to grow. This is a time of semi-dormancy when the plants are half asleep. Allow the soil almost to dry out between waterings and then give only sufficient water to maintain and nurture life, moisturizing the soil without making it totally wet.

The golden rule at any time, particularly in winter is never water when the soil is wet.

Make a practice of watering early in the day and drain off all the surplus water before replacing the plant in position.

Rule of hand Watering Tips

In winter, you need to water the intermediate and delicate varieties with tepid water – at room temperature: 21°C or 70°F. This treatment will also benefit the easy varieties. Mollycoddling your houseplants in winter, which usually means overwatering often, has fatal results. It is better to neglect them a little.

When the room temperature drops sharply at night, especially during cold weather, always remove a plant that is moist or wet to a warmer position. Plants left on windowsills, between the curtains and the window, are in great danger of being damaged or killed by frost. Always bring them into the room and night.

Drooping leaves is usually a sign of excessive dryness. Never follow a period of dryness with heavy watering, as this is going to cause the loss of the lower leaves. Return gradually to normal watering.

Brown and black patches of wet on the leaves or stem are often a sign of overwatering in winter. If the lower parts of the stem are affected, your plant is possibly going to die. If the leaves are affected, keep the plant almost dry for a while. Some leaves are going to fall, but the life of the plant may be saved.

Going for a long holiday – What about my indoor plants?

I know about avid gardeners who have not had a holiday for years, because they are so worried about their plants. I wonder with all their experience, they did not think of common sense tips which are going to help keep their plants healthy and happy during their sojourn on a vacation.

Before going away for any length in spring or summer water all the houseplants thoroughly. Insert two small stakes in each pot. They should be slightly taller than the plant, one at each side of the pot.

Slip a polythene bag over the stakes and secure it to the pot with a rubber band. Place the plants in a position where they will not be exposed to strong sunlight. Moisture will then evaporate from the leaves, condense on the walls of the polythene bag and run down to the bottom of the bag, where it will be absorbed by the water again.

The plants will be in their ideal atmosphere with the humidity and a simple, self-watering device which you can describe as a miniature greenhouse.

Feeding Your Plants

Feeding is beneficial during the period of active growth from spring through summer to early autumn. In late autumn and winter discontinue feeding altogether.

There are many good brands of houseplant fertilizers available from florists or horticultural nursery men. Always follow the makers instructions because if you exceed this stated dosage, you may harm your plant.

Small bottles of liquid fertilizers are perhaps the most convenient to use in the home.

A few drops in the water, according to the manufacturer's instructions, and you are going to have adequate feeding when watering.

I really like this informative URL, which gives me plenty of information on organic fertilizers. I definitely do not prefer chemicals in my garden.

http://www.motherearthnews.com/organic-gardening/liquid-fertilizers-zm0z11zhun.aspx

Many an experienced houseplant enthusiasts fall into one common trap. If the plant appears unhealthy, they think that it is starving. Try to determine first whether the symptoms are due to damage by cold, or watering or even excessive dryness.

If the possibilities can be excluded and if the roots are healthy and not damaged then feed the plant, but remember that feeding a sick plant will make it worse.

If the leaves are green and pale, then you need to feed it. That is going to be the pot is full of roots.

Re-potting a plant

Why do you need to repot a plant? This is often necessary, when you find your plant growing really large, and the container seems to be rather small, and inadequate to contain all that growth. But if you planted it in the initial stages in a large pot, especially one which gives it a lot of room to grow, you may not need to re-pot it again.

Most kinds are happy to live in pots, which may appear too small for them, and there are also plants that have filled their containers with roots and they are going to live there happily if they are fed regularly.

Late spring or early summer is the right time for repotting a plant as the roots then have time to become established in the new soil before the cold weather sets in.

Top heaviness should be the main indication for repotting. But before repotting, you need to inspect the soil. This can be done by spreading the fingers of one hand on either side of the stem between the lower leaves and the top of the pot. You can also spread the fingers of one hand around the stem of the plant and invert the pot.

Tap the rim sharply two or three times. This is because the soil has been loosened and the ball of soil emerges intact.

Stand the soil ball on a layer of potting compost in a larger pot, so that the top is 1 inch below the rim.

Level the surface of the soil and water the plant only sparingly for 3 to 4 weeks after repotting. If the roots are obviously overcrowded or tangled round the outside of the soil ball, you will need to repot into a one size larger pot.

Cover the drainage hole of a larger pot with crocks, put some potted compost in the bottom, stand the soil ball in the center, then fill up with potted compost and firm down.

If repotting is unnecessary, drop the ball back into the same pot and tap the base sharply once or twice. The plant should then be firmly in place, but if it is not, firm the soil with both your thumbs.

What Is the Best Potting Mixture

I would suggest any potting mixture which is made up of compost with the addition of one third part by volume of leaf mold and peat. Look for good standard compost, available from most florists and horticultural experts. Any peaty compost can suffice as long as it has an open porous texture.

I would recommend a potting compost for indoor houseplants with this combination – two parts rich loamy soil with turf, 1 ½ parts leaf mold, one washed sand, 1/4 part farmyard manure and half part peat by volume.

This is going to be slightly acid with a pH of 5.5 – six.

This potting mixture and the pot ball of the plan should be just moist. Water sparingly for a few weeks to encourage the roots to grow into the new soil.

Never repot a sick plant whose roots have been damaged by bad watering or cold. This is the surest way to kill it.

Training and Pruning Your Plants

In the winter months houseplants tend to make thin, long, weak growth with small leaves. In the spring when vigorous growth resumes, this poor growth should be cut back as far as the good-sized healthy leaves to improve the appearance and shape of your plant. Healthier and more robust side shoots will soon begin to grow.

The climbing and trailing varieties with variegated leaves are easily going to revert to green leaves during the winter. That is because the light is inadequate. In spring, this green growth should be cut back to the last well variegated leaf in order to encourage variegated side shoots.

If a plant is growing too tall and you want it to growing a bushy shape, stop the growing shoots by pinching out the tips. This encourages the growth of side shoots and you are soon going to have a Bush.

Houseplants are frequently seen trained up trellises and bamboo supports to form partial screens between two parts of a large room. The climbing and the trailing varieties are going to lend them extremely well to this practical and decorated use of indoor plants.

Climbers love to grow around moss takes. Within florists wire, you can bind a stake of moist moss around a stake leaving only the pointed end of the stake free. Drive this end into the soil in the pot so that the stake stands firm and upright and tie the plant loosely to the stake.

When the plant is watered, let some water trickle down the stake to keep the moss damp. Some climbing plants, particularly members of the arum family produce aerial roots in the damp moss. Find a pliable stake somewhat taller than the plant so that you can allow for growth. 1 inch layer of moss – sphagnum moss – should be bound around this stay, before you drive it upright. The aerial roots are going to cling into the damp moss.

Cleaning Your Plants

Regular spraying of the leaves with tepid water helps to prevent any attacks by insect pests and also provides the necessary wash that indoor plants cannot get from rain.

I heard about a five-star hotel in Harare, about 20 years ago, where the leaves were sponged with equal mixtures of milk and water. This gave them a gloss. In the same way you can sponge it with beer, and you are going to get the same effect, but you're going to get a beery atmosphere.

In the 60s, it was fashionable to spray the leaves with aerosol spray. This left a thin, dust resistant film of plastic to the surface of the leaves. This spray was used only tough smooth leaved plants and particularly improved the appearance of rubber plants outdoors. But as I am more eco-conscious, I know that the spray is going to harm me. Anything which leaves a plastic deposit on the surface of the leaf is going to leave that same deposit on my respiratory system. So milk and water for me!

Clean the hairy leaves of such varieties with a soft brush, such as a paint brush or blow off accumulated dust with a handheld vacuum cleaner. The same treatment is recommended, or the leaves of silvery gray varieties with scales. These scales form the attractive silvery bands on many members of the pineapple family *Aechmea rhodocyanea* and can be rubbed off really easily, so that the appearance of the plant is spoiled.

Common pests and their treatment

Be it never so indoors, there is no place like home for pests. The best preventive measure is sponging the upper and underside of the leaves regularly.

If there are earthworms in the soil, encourage them. They are not pests. Earthworms are happy in rich organic loamy soil with a little bit of sand in it.

Here are some easy ways in which you can recognize the pests and control them.

I do not know about the efficacy of saltwater and tobacco water to get rid of these pests. Some of my friends say that it is very effective for getting rid of household pests, especially on plants. But I know that salt is detrimental to the health of the soil. Tobacco is detrimental to my own health in any form, including water, smoke, and powder. So I'm not going to try any of these out.

Pest	Control
Green fly – This is the most common pest. It is going to enter through open windows or it can be brought in on cut flowers during spring and summer. Green fly cluster on young shoots and prevent normal growth	Spray with liquid derris, which is not poisonous. This is the climbing leguminous plant native to New Guinea. Remember to remove any aquariums from the room before you try this treatment.
Red spider – This is called red spider, but it is very rarely the red in color. It attacks we underside of the leaves, particularly in	Same treatment as in Green fly.

dry and hot conditions. The affected leaves first appears scattered with little yellow spots and later become brittle and dry.	
Scale insect – These are small insects shaped like shields with waxy shells. These cling to the underside of the leaves mainly on shrubby plants. You can recognize their presence by a black sticky deposits on the surface of the leaves below. That is the waste from a scale insect	Wipe them off with damp cloths. If they are difficult to dislodge push them off with your thumbnail
Whiteflies – these are tiny moth like flies which appear in great numbers	Same treatment as in green flies and red spiders.
Mealy bugs – small insects with white covering found mainly in stem joints and on the underside of leaves.	Wipe them off with damp cloth.

Appendix

Index of common names and botanical names of popular houseplants.

http://www.houseplantsexpert.com/a-z-list-of-house-plants.html

Author Bio

Dueep Jyot Singh is a Management and IT Professional who managed to gather Postgraduate qualifications in Management and English and Degrees in Science, French and Education while pursuing different enjoyable career options like being an hospital administrator, IT,SEO and HRD Database Manager/ trainer, movie scriptwriter, theatre artiste and public speaker, lecturer in French, Marketing and Advertising, ex-Editor of Hearts On Fire (now known as Solstice) Books Missouri USA, advice columnist and cartoonist, publisher and Aviation School trainer, ex- moderator on Medico.in, banker, student councilor ,travelogue writer … among other things! One fine morning, she decided that she had enough of killing herself by Degrees and went back to her first love -- writing. It's more enjoyable! She already has 48 published academic and 14 fiction- in- different- genre books under her belt.

When she is not designing websites or making Graphic design illustrations for clients , she is browsing through old bookshops hunting for treasures, of which she has an enviable collection – including R.L. Stevenson, O.Henry, Dornford Yates, Maurice Walsh, C.N.Williamson, Sapper, Bartimeus and the crown of her collection- Dickens "The Old Curiosity Shop," and so on… Just call her "Renaissance Woman") - collecting herbal remedies, acting like Universal Helping Hand/Agony Aunt, or escaping to her dear mountains for a bit of exploring, collecting herbs and plants and trekking.

Check out some of the other JD-Biz Publishing books

Gardening Series on Amazon

Health Learning Series

Learn To Draw Series

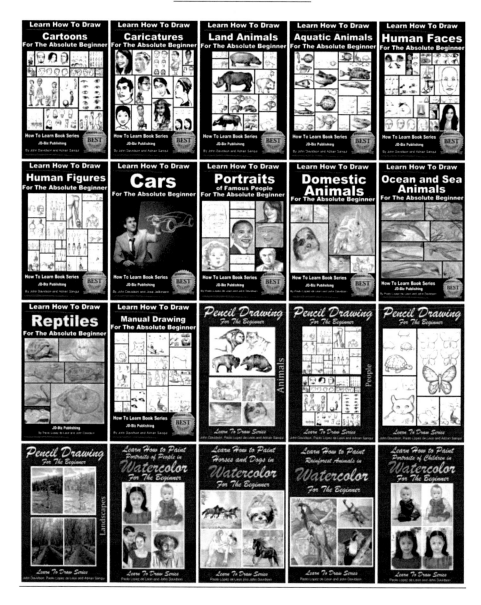

How to Build and Plan Books

Entrepreneur Book Series

Our books are available at

1. Amazon.com

2. Barnes and Noble

3. Itunes

4. Kobo

5. Smashwords

6. Google Play Books

Download Free Books!

http://MendonCottageBooks.com

Publisher

JD-Biz Corp

P O Box 374

Mendon, Utah 84325

http://www.jd-biz.com/

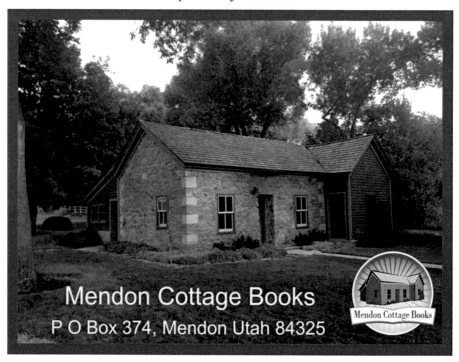

Made in the USA
Middletown, DE
03 January 2016